Crisis Mode

A poetry collection

Danielle Koch

BookLeaf Publishing
India | USA | UK

Made with ❤ on the BookLeaf Publishing Platform
www.bookleafpub.in
www.bookleafpub.com

Dedication

For my family.
For my friends.
For Marshall.

All of my love,

Dani

Preface

"Crisis Mode" came about from a time in my life in which I was operating in a state of perpetual stress. I wanted to write about my experience, my emotions, and my thinking patterns in a way that others would understand and could relate. This time in my life was the second time I was hospitalized, and second time I took on intensive out-patient therapy. I thought I was done with these problems, but they kept circling back to me until I actually dealt with them. During this period, I learned how to actually take care of myself. Not merely doing activities that appear like self-care. Self-care looked like setting boundaries with people, proceeding in relationships one step at a time, and focusing first on myself. All of these ideas are not new, not revolutionary, but to actually learn how to impliment these practices in my life was transformative. I was able to get myself out of crisis mode, into the growth zone. Each day still presents its own challenge, and its own gift. And if I look carefully enough, many times, they are one and the same.

Danielle Koch is an English teacher living in the Minneapolis area. She still goes to therapy. And she does yoga, reads, and writes in community with others.

Acknowledgements

To everyone who has ever been in treatment or in group with me.

This is for us.
The weirdos.
The heritics.
The sensitive souls.
The neurodiverse.

And anyone who has ever fallen down in the same hole, again, and again.
And again. But can't see a way around it.

Yet.

May you hold onto this possibility:
Healing is just around the corner.

1. Spinning

I can't get control
Can't find the thread
Can't locate
What I was thinking of?

It just takes over.
And I lay frozen on the couch.
Or shuttering in tears
paralyzed by fear
worried about my own survival.

Will I make it until this evening?
Who could I even call who would not respond with an
air
of disappointment?
I've been trying so hard to not
to not disappoint everyone.
To be the person that people believe
I should be.

The accommodating one
Putting my needs on hold
Rising to the occasion
To not let everyone see

Just what this is doing to me.

I'm having a panic attack every day
And just barely recovering over the weekend.
I'm not seeing sun, touching grass.
Not bending to my will.

I am broken.
I am helpless.
I'm so afraid of coming out of the shadows and being
real
real about just how fucking hard it is.

And stopping
Stopping the spin.
Dropping everything.
Finding a safeplace.
Where I can slow down my mind
And find just where my brain dropped that thought.
And pick up the thread again.

2. This bitch?

Newly diagnosed,
I emerge from the hospital with one of those
draw-string bags they make you put your
belongings in when you check in.
The moment you put on scrubs.
Suddenly you're not a person anymore.
You're a patient in a ward with other mentally ill people.

Apparently, you don't have to wear scrubs
Just make sure you remove your laces
belts, hoodie ties.
My hair lies flat against my head–no true replacement
products,
Just this super coconutty curl cream
That makes my hair more staticy and simultaneously
oily.

I feel everything, raw
like it's written on my bones.
I'm shaking. Not sure which
direction Mom should drive to.

I realize I need to go home and get my laptop either way.
I point straight ahead, and mom makes the lane change.

I take a beat outside my apartment. Mom turns off the engine.

I take a deep breath, not sure if I can make it inside, get what I need and split.
I'm not sure of anything, anything except the eyes
and judgments of the world upon me.
I turn the key in the door and Mom holds it open
I throw my green draw-string bag over my shoulder like a sack and head inside.
The red carpet makes the hallway
ominous and narrow at the end.
I turn my key, awaiting the smell of weeks' old dishes and trash.

Instead, I smell dusty air.
Mom wasn't kidding when she said she and Dad cleaned up my place.
Inside, I grab my laptop and immediately send some emails.
The guilt of being out a week
plus the three that wait in the wings
haunt me.
Enough dread and doubt to weigh my feet down
like cement shoes.

That's how the mob used to get rid of rats,

pour cement over their shoes, let it harden
And drop them to sink to the depths.
Maybe that will be my fate too.
The bitch who couldn't hack the last month of school.

The girl whose body effectively gave out on her,
whose brain melted between her ears.
The harder my self-betrayal clings to me, the faster I
sink.

At the moment, my shoulders relax.
Mom has been on her phone all this time.
Everything has stopped and I can look at her.
It doesn't look like she slept very well.
But she doesn't yawn, doesn't complain.

In the hospital, I realized that I can't care about anything
more than I care
About myself.
And I know the problem in this equation is
me.
My mom looks at me and asks what I want to do.
Do I want to stay? Head to her house?
I said I wanted to stay here.
But I need groceries first, and to figure out something for
dinner.
I don't remember what I went out to get that night. And

I don't remember many of the nights after.

I couldn't have anticipated many events to follow.
My principal's reaction to taking three weeks off.
And attempting sub-plans for the rest of the year.
The conversation with that friend
That made me want to slide out of my skin.
And surprising support.

I open the bag and take out my
Homemade Depression Daddy flip flops
Freeing the chapped toes at the grocery store.
This bitch has got to eat, if nothing else.

3. Imposter Syndrome

Look at me.
Look at me!
LOOK at ME, but not too closely.
I want you to acknowledge this person
The one that I'm trying
Trying so, so hard
To be.
I'm forcing this corset to fit
To make me acceptable, approachable, accommodating
slice of me that you're so comfortable receiving.
But I secretly want you to understand
this struggle. The work. The unbearable weight of
self-imposed silence.

Please don't respond softly with compassion,
Nor sweetly with understanding.
That's honestly not what I deserve.
I can't force it anymore if I tried.
The fitting in, sticking it out, and powering through.
I have nothing to put forth, to make it to the end.

What mask should I wear today?
What emotions do I need to feel right now?
I'm trying to shield judgements, with armor made of

feathers.
I know that I'm not perfect.
And that trying to be is a fucking waste of time.
Life's a journey, not a destination.
Growth isn't about arriving anywhere.
Yes, I've been told.

But without this effort, without this grind, maybe I
don't know who I am.
Maybe you too would see through
Only if curiosity about me
overcame you
Enough to look
Only then, you'd acknowledge the smoke and mirrors
The spell of myself that I'm trying to cast.
I am an illusionist. I cast spells and create enchantments.
A Witch since childhood.
Obsessed with moods, cycles,
predictability, stories with a comfortable narrative
closure.
But I want to stop this work
Of shielding myself.

I don't want to feel fake, vague, or empty.
There's nothing to cure, there is no mistake.
I am all there is. And yet it's never enough.
I'm painting the picture of me and I keep running out of

product.
Where do you go to get more of yourself?

Somewhere in me, I know.
I know that I don't need to become someone else,
or live an extraordinary life to be loved.
I know I need to stop squishing me
Let me take up space, to breathe and sing
the song of myself
Or so it goes.
But to do that around others and not know how I'd be
received is
Enormous.
I know it's my responsibility to
revive myself back to living.
And not just take up the performance of myself.

I don't need a standing ovation,
and yet it would be incredibly validating if you gave
the role of myself 100% on Rotten Tomatoes.
Seriously, grade my paper.
See how much work that I've put in?

Yet time has etched itself on my skin and has
hassled me from the spaces that I could have
done such good work in.
I don't appreciate being bullied, but I feel deserving of it.

There're so many threadbare ends of the person that I'm trying to become.
It's not the person who's trying to enchant you right now.
Maybe approval of my efforts is not what I'm looking for
I actually don't need you to like me.

I've kept running into the same walls, maybe because I can't admit
I can't grow into a different being.
I can't body-switch.
But I'm ready to give.
Give the gift of life and all the pleasures, sorrows, and ambiguity
to me. So I won't be someone else's answer.

4. The mirror

I look at myself – as if
for the first time.

I see…
the half moons
where none were.
Not the last time
I checked.

I run my fingers through
my hair.
Pulling and peeling strands
as dry as a broom bristles
uncontained.
Too defiant to bow down to
the great gobs of conditioner
now stuck to the back of my hair.
Now layered sticky and limp –
really needing to be washed
again.

Washing anything takes an enormous force of will
Now there's
no reserves

No one replacing my 24/7 vigil against the darkness

How am I really doing?
What does my crisis mode look like?

It's like I'm
a soldier stranded without her company –
in a torrential downpour –
With enemies on all sides –
terrified – to – shoot

not knowing
who or what
I'll

hit

or if I'll recognize the faces of friends
or The Enemy

The mirror does not utter a word
but that bitch does not hold back.
It shows me to myself
and shows me just how I've been taking care
of her.
Turns out living this way is not invisible to the body

Bloodshot eyes,

chapped lips,
flaking skin.
Doing anymore than a single step
Is not –
Will –
Not

No,

Not willpower.

But love
Meds
Food
Sleep
Sun
Saying "no"

Will help me climb out of crisis mode
Steal the mirror from the bitch who points it all out
And reunite it with the friend who
Won't talk smack.

So you didn't sleep last night?
It's ok, it's Sunday.

Take your meds and
go back to bed.

5. I forgive

I forgive myself.
For everything I had to do
to get to
now.
To be here
at this point.

At least
I know that I can breathe

– short – gasps –

in – out – in. Shaky

tears release
and pour down.
My eyes see clearer
Now.

After I have un-
clenched, un-
earthed, un-
did thoughts
Of killing

myself.

I forgive.

6. That friend

You're that friend who drags it out of me.
Even when I'm not ready. Even and especially when I'm crying.
I don't want people to see me cry.
Despite all precautions – over the phone and all –
You hear me cry.
I don't want people to hear me.
Me. Just me. Raw and hurting.

You want to know. NEED to know.
Want me to know that you're my friend and
You love me.

Terrified, exposed, and on display;
A target painted on my open chest.
Talking to you so directly about my pain
burns me up inside.

Should I feel like my body has gone through a meat grinder?
Are you really my friend — when I feel
this way after I hang up?

I told you why–

it's hard to trust people, why–
I need to hear from you.
That I believe that if you don't reach out, then I'm not
important to you,
so you shouldn't be important to me. And maybe you
never were.

Did I overshare? Did I let you down?
Did I make you feel sorry for me?
I didn't mean to. I merely illustrated
why this was so fucking hard for me.

Not simply life in general, but this –
talking to you face to face.
That's really what's going on.

Continuing to speak truth
        through the discomfort.
                                        On display – all feelings
out

helpless and apart

                It's all my hurt and now... you know.
What comes next?

To me this conversation reeks like conflict.

To me this attention is like
having my skin singed off.

Let me make you laugh with this irony –
I am the mastermind of my private misery.

Let me make you think deeply, or spot something...
over there!
So I can hide once again in the version of me
I'm most comfortable being
with you. For you.
So you'll never have to know,
Because I didn't want you to.

You're saying that you're my friend and you love me
That you'd want to help me if you can.

Still, I can't tell anyone. NO. because then they'd find
out.
Because then they'd be disappointed in me. Like you.

How do I tell you that I'm drowning when I'm gasping
for air?
I don't have gills.
Now it's my fault I didn't reach out.
How can I tell that I'm the bottom of a hole?
I'd been told, for 20 years, that I was at the bottom of a

lake.
And for some reason, I've imagined the water the entire time.

Do you bring out the worst in me?
Do I?

Yes, you love me.
But you saying you love me upsets me.

No, your love doesn't make me sad.
It's simply an idea that I've never felt, never taken it in from you, friend.
Yes, that's all on me. But my perceptions are cutting and I have long receipts of disappointed evenings, rain checks on sunny days.

I shrink my world smaller.
How do I know you love me when you don't respond to my texts?
Was it out of line to call? How do I trust you'll answer an emergency?
Why in the hell do you want to be around me?
Do you still like me? Am I likable?

Today,
I told you that I woke up to my life and saw that

I haven't been living.
I soldiered on with life's obligations.

And I don't feel loved because
I don't let you love me
I don't let you take care of me.
So I can't heal.

And I need you to be with me to help me.
I need you to love me.
I need to love you.
You're That Friend –

But then you're unavailable when you said you would be
Free.
I can't call when you
talk both sides of anything
and make me feel more vulnerable– and less known.

My paranoia isn't without evidence.
Can't call it crazy. You lit the gas yourself.

When could I have asked for help?
I've been describing and speaking up about how I've
been doing, struggling.
You knew.
You knew and let me fall.

You're that friend.

And now that I'm out of the hospital, you want to say...
That I'm your friend and you love me.

So, when could've I asked for help?
For your help?

How can I depend on you when you've got a 100 things to do.
and that makes you feel good.
It prevents me from asking.
You have a tone like a boss, not a friend.
When we were all busy with our own things.
There is no help, I know.

How could I have asked for help
When I didn't knowI needed help
Until it was too late
Until I had to get out

Now with new knowledge
A fresh perspective, new diagnosis, new meds...
I'm becoming a healthier me.

Now the question is –
How much help from you do I need?

Can I be around you as I'm piecing myself back together?

Yes, you're That Friend.

But, do I want you to be?

7. Trust

"Trust."
she said,
"Trust yourself."
And then my brain told me to kill myself.
And then I had an urge to get the knife.

Trust myself? How do I learn to
do that again?
Unanswered questions spin and pluck
scary thoughts.
I don't want to be one of those Sylvias, or Virginias
women who lose it to fire, water...
Elements out of their control.

"Trust."
She said.
"Trust the process."
And then she said, "It works if you work it."
And then she said, "It just takes time."

Take your meds.
    Get fresh air.
    Eat a full meal.
    Call a friend.

Read a book.
Use your skills.
Get a good night's rest.

Rinse and repeat until
until,
(wait for it)
the meds start working.

The waves of Self keep taking me down.
I can't live –
the rest of the story when —-
I am caught on the cliff–
hanger.

Adrenaline ensures a sharp nosedive, every time.

I am not a Boeing plane. I am not fated to go down.
And yet, I don't know my limits.
I'm learning, resetting the onboarding instructions.
Using the elements nearby to guide me.

Wind – my momentum forward.
Earth – my grounding and direction.
Now, where to land?
Where to go until the meds start?
Until I start

start over.

8. Disembodied head

Sometimes I forget that I have
a body. That I am
a body. That I live my life through
a body. My body.

I forget the tension between my shoulders,
the sore spot in my sit bones,
the way my belly button moves up and down,
abdomen filling with air. The sound of
exhalation, like a contained wind
vibrating through my nostrils.

I forget how very much like the sea I am.
The waves crashing on land echo the way
my breath does, as my pulse stills and steadies.
In two three, out two three.
In two three, sigh it out.

I am called in a lot of ways to respond faster than
my rhythm. Really, I am called out.
I am put on the spot. To give a quick answer so that
numbers can be given, and I can be counted.
Or more often than not, counted upon.

I have to hold–

–my

–

–breath.

Stop the flow of oxygen to my brain. And react

on instinct.

Yes.

No.

I have lost. Lost the feeling of feet upon the earth.

Lost the steady stream of breath.

Forgotten that I am more than

my ability to answer in the affirmative.

That I am mightier than any twinge of guilt

that pollutes my waters.

I am bigger than what I can

do for other people.

Selfless

Not only the opposition of selfish

But it implies a loss of self

of abandonment

of disconnection.

Disempowered because

I disembodied.

I forgot where I stood.

I lost track of my birthright.
My autonomy over not just
my choices, my life,
but moment to moment safety
grounded in my own body.

How do I fight back when
more of the same bombardment
always comes. A quick interruption.
A notification that sucks my attention away

When I can't just say no.
Because you can't always just say
No.
Maybe I'll reprogram my YES into a I'll GET BACK TO YOU.
Or A LET ME THINK ABOUT IT.
Or A NOT RIGHT NOW.

Now let me return to these winds
of breath. Let me go back to silence.
And allow myself to feel once again
all of me.

9. Cognitive dissonance

The very thought that proves your whole existence
wrong.
I felt okay yesterday. And I ate three and a half hours
ago
And my body craves food again. I'm sick of all the food I
have.
Maybe a muffin I stuffed in the freezer. That would be
decent.

Tonight and tomorrow, I'm meeting friends.
It's such work to get ahold of people, make plans, follow
through
Be present with them, and rinse and repeat.
But simultaneously, my brain hums with anticipation
Glows with delight
Almost like a fanfare of trumpets in my head, and racers
have started.
At the moment, accessing that place is easy.

And afterwards, I wonder what they thought of me.
Was I too much? Did I hold too much in and back?

The truth is other people's opinions of me are none of
my business.

She was right. I do need to speak up when I'm
struggling.
However, I also needed to keep up with the charade of
professionalism
and to offer an olive branch of trust,
There is truth in there was never any place to confide in–
with her.
And no, I'm not seeing her. Message received.
What she offered, she couldn't deliver. And she knew it.

But what I want, what I want is all that Marshall has and
can give.
Or maybe not. Maybe I want to explore this side of
letting love in.
And not be so consumed by it.

Tears happened at therapy today. Talking about fear.
Fear of being consumed by things that I love. Letting
them swallow me up
And drown in their intensity.

I want to ride on top of them, like a wave.
Not caught underneath, or wrapped up in the tide
that tosses me back and forth.

10. Car thoughts

What if I get into an accident,
That way, I'd be laid up in the
Hospital and not have to
Teach for a few days.
I could just take the wrong
exit, get lost
And be an hour late.
But then, I'd be late and my contract time
Has technically already started.
And I'm still in my car.
Now parked. About to have the day
Start.
Do I want to leave the
Safety of silence
And enter the din of willfulness?
Move through each hour
Guiding and correcting,
Mirroring and mentoring?

What if I run out?
What if my tank is low
Or I haven't changed the oil
In a while?

This miracle of arriving
Showing up
About to grit a smile
And do it anyway
is for me.

Without me, nothing gets done.
With me, something will.
I'm meeting the moment
With whatever I have left
to give, and offer up more than that
Willingly.

But on my way home,
I'll try to avoid the necessity
Of self. Maybe I'll over do
And perfect.
Not care for her.
She just wants some
Peace. She wasn't
Ready to give all that she had
And I shouldn't expect her to
be. Teacher, teach her
How to care for
herself. Not to destroy
herself. Or let herself be
so depleted without

filling up again.

How can, how about when
The deadline inevitably gets
Pushed back–
So therefore goes the self
To be shelved for another
day.

Start your
engines. It's time to do it
All over again.

You can't look back to what was.
Only out to what will be.
Giving it all out
Again, digging out the well to
Give more.
Water, water everywhere,
But none for me to drink.

11. I'm having a panic attack.

I'm having a
panic attack.
No, I know I'm not
Dying. I'm not being that
Dramatic. I just know
I'll never be all right
Again. Now that I've
Realized what this is
I can take my PRN
And wait. Call out
To the panic, by its name.
Rumplestillskin, say it
Three times and he appears.
Say I'm having a panic attack three times and
Suddenly I'm able to ride
it out. Let the storm
ensue. Let my ship
Get wrecked. Because I can
See the eye of the storm.
The light is almost
Here. I'm having a
Panic attack.
Let my breathing slow

And the villain will appear.
Rumplestiltskin of my mind
My dear old anxieties have
Thwarted me
Once again.
I will not go down with
the ship.
But I'll get up again
Tomorrow
And know my panic
Has not claimed me
yet.

12. Stuck

Stuck on my back
Like a tortoise. Flipped flapjack.
I can't will myself
To turn over
To raise up would be like
Raising the dead.
What would even be the pont?
Time inevitably goes
That direction
Towards entropy.
So why not scroll
And binge and remain
Trapped under the weight
Of my mind.
There's no getting up
Until someone offers
To pick me up and lay me
Down
Right side up.

13. Stretch.

Stretch and release. Steady my beating heart. Shhhh.
Calm down. Sigh with the pur of the cat. Lie as a listless dog.
Be still now. Your time has come. It's no time to react.

Feel the space
the echo in the response. Settle in the resonance your strings strum
Feel the reverie of melody,
the movement still on your bones.

Unlatch the hooks around your lungs.
The ones you didn't inflate completely.
You didn't let yourself breathe until now. Until you can really release.
Really feel the air go in and out. Inhale and exhale. Open and close.

Open and close. Come in from the storm, your time has come.
It's time for a break. It's time to appreciate what has and what will be.
Be in the moment.
Check out. It's time to create

liminal space.

Come back to yourself.
To the arms that have been waiting to hold.
You. Fitting you, cradling around, encircling, the
precious body that's been holding
it together all day. Let you be you.

Give yourself space for once. All your bones
are so tired–worn from configuring the space,
giving the commands,
modeling what other young bodies must do in our
shared space.

That one who has all eyes on her.
The one that must be clothed and behave.
The one that must think and wholeheartedly respond.
The one who has to be, has to occupy, has to be whole,
now.
Can't be absent-minded
or distracted or dreamy or flowy or prickly or off or on a
mental holiday.
Must do until it is done.
Must ready herself for the fledgling march forward.
Must soldier on.

But at the end of the day,

the armor must come off, and not just off,
you have to breathe, move, sleep, and lie your whole person down.
Your whole self–all the parts that you've set aside.

All of the places that you've tucked up inside and have not stretched,
Not listened enchanted with the voices taking hold,
in the power that comes to the surface, once you're quiet.
Now you're present to the spirits possessing you.

And maybe tonight is just lying in wait. And maybe tonight is practicing,
modeling what it would be like for the real thing to show up and ignite.
Lighting some candles and waiting for the good spirits to rush in–and overtake the space that you make.

14. Medicated and it feels so

Medicated and it feels so
clear. I have new labels.
Really, it's the acronyms that do the work for me.

Some say it's female embodied ADHD.
Others say I have Quiet BPD. But can anything quiet and feminine
Be so torturous? So cruel? Such a willful master?
It's almost like these labels make it feel like a less serious diagnosis.
That it's almost a "normal" female thing, with more than a bit of a slant.
Coloring outside of the lines instead of in.

For the first time, I don't mind these labels.
My tendency to shift into black or white thinking
My pattern of procrastination, a heavy dose of avoidance.
Making the mountains bigger without any attempt to climb them.

But with meds, not because I'm relying solely on their influence,
I've done the work,

I've breathed life into myself. And came out O.K.
I'm far from perfect. My brain just functions differently.

So I guess I'm a bit atypical. That doesn't make me any less.
In some scenarios, it makes me more. More.
More fantastic. More ambitious. More lovable.
Because there are simply more things in my mind and heart to love.

To get here, I needed to be medicated.
To get here, I needed therapy.
To get here, I needed to give myself time, movement, sunshine, water.

I've been able to rise to this occasion.
To paint myself the colors I want to be, not the ones I feel that I have to be.
I feel lighter. I don't feel as if I have to try so hard.
I don't have to anticipate everything.
And I don't need to.

I can stand tall in the midst of all of these things.
I am solid.
I am a mountain.
No matter what my red boulders are made of
And if they have extra scars or dirt.

I no longer sink.
I no longer fall to my frailties. I let them wrap around me.
Let me hug you. Let me claim you. Let me name you.

It doesn't mean I don't have faults, or these things don't affect me.
But I've stopped unraveling.
I am grateful for all of these things and what they've done for me.
But now I don't need to try so hard, struggle so much, armor up my
Tense grin to keep the sharks at bay.

I'm thankful for all the ways I've learned to survive,
To fight, to fail, to succeed. But I don't need that program any more.
I am free. I am released.
I am me.

15. With you

With you
at the edge,
toes in the water,
hands clasped.
The sun passes behind
the clouds.
I nuzzle you.

This is before.
Before my mouth has
known yours.
Before we held each other
naked in my lavender sheets.
The wind picks up
And I slide my feet between
yours.
I don't feel cold in your
arms.
You lean in and
this won't be the
last time our lips
meet.
The ducks inch around us.
People pass on their runs,

out to play basketball,
to take pictures in the
golden hour.
But we don't see them.
All we know is the inches
of lips, the curl of
your cupid's bow. The edge of
my tongue.
The way we can know each other, like this.
Just here, with you.
Before.

16. Creator

Sometimes to be considered art, you need to be
more than a little conservative.
My performance of you can be on the sword's edge
of making sense. Substance constructed into pristine
form.
Sliced and constrained marble.
Having smoothed down your edges.
Trampled down your substance, now beginning to piece
you together.

You are my ragdoll, both form and flop.
Let me speak through you.
Will you let me?
Will you bend and not break?
Won't you let me speak for you?
Speak through your molten metal,
clay,
primordial ooze and
surrender to this
spector's artful manipulation.

Am I kind?
Is God kind in beginning of the universe,
setting time in motion?

I have all power over you.

It's necessary
to bewitch you.
Don't you agree?
I see through what you are and
can birth possibility to reality.

I envision your possibilities, your answers,
your fulfillment, your story.

Before you were just sitting there.
Plain, unused,
Silent.

And now you're animated,
delighted by the process.
Or is that my emotion pouring through you?
Isn't that me making you come alive.
Imbued with spirit, and soul.

Do I have the right?
I think because I can, that I am.
I have permission to create because I am a human being.
It's the action of creation that calls inspiration.
And you are held up as example–

You exist.

And I made you.

17. Contented

I am whole
In this moment
In this moment able to
articulate my thoughts
and put them down.

The sun is shining,
There's a breeze through the windows
Skimming across my bare legs

On the whole,
I am comfortable.
Tension lingers in my body.
But I am able to feel it
While eavesdropping on the birds
cawing, chirping, cooing.
I crunch and release my shoulders

In this moment,
My kitchen, between my two windows
Seeing the breeze sway the leaves.
Languorous.
Not my mind

My eyes close.
And just listen.

18. Longing

It's a howl from deep within.
It's a sharp chasm of time, a void with a wind blowing through
End to end, vast like the Gobi
There is no edge to this
It feels like I can slip off the plane and fall in
I end up in the wanting
Like craving the warmth of summer sun in a blizzard
The images and memories of having, possessing,
being overcome by love
tickled by joy
refreshed by peace
satisfied by meaning, purpose, and drive.
And now I'm famished and nothing around will satisfy
This hunger, that's more than anything my mouth can call out
Sustenance of this kind doesn't just materialize
It must be worked for, drilled into one's life and the opportunities will come
But until I have what I need to do the work
I'll always go to bed
Empty.

19. Spoons

You start with three
Going to need to wash
One to get through the day.
Maybe a nap will do.
Can't sleep, you're left
With two. Cancel plans,
free up your evening.
You still have to do the day.
Eat some beef jerky,
Fill up on caffeine.
Gargle mouthwash,
Stumble out the door.
You have one spoon remaining.
Not enough to dig yourself out
Of the hole you're in.

One spoon gets you to work.
You're into the red spoons
at work. You're now borrowing
From the weekend. That's time to
Hunker down, order out, sleep and
Not do the dishes. And slowly recoup
Your spoons for the next week.

Tomorrow, you start with five. Barely enough.
But starting to get to enough is an accomplishment
Worthy of washing three spoons to use to celebrate
With friends. The slow revival of self,
The unearthing of willpower, the flame
finally found the wick, now flickering again.
Don't blow too hard or use
Those spoons too rashly. Starting over isn't
An option right now.

What is rationing, conserving,
In the hayday of optimism?
The golden era is over too
Quickly anyway.

You have the number you have.
And sure, you can wash them
But washing takes spoons you don't have.
So sit tight, and do what
You only can.
The work of existing
And performing
A life you'd wish
Was worth living.

How many spoons to feel better?
How many are dirty?

Take account before overdrafting your
Willpower and don't forget
To breathe through it
When you run out.

20. Weather dependent

Moods. Up and down.
Bright and overcast,
Dreary to dreamy.

May the sky change its
Mind about my day.
May it hold me up
In the way only clouds
Can.
And not burst.

Otherwise, I don't know
If I can weather
this weather.
Or is the weather
dependent on me,
in some small
self-flagellating
way?

Won't you just be
70 and sunny?
Today and tomorrow.
Is that so hard?

Don't let my SADS
Come out in the summer.
When the sun overwhelms
and the heat stiffles.
Don't let me suffer the dog-days in
silence.

I'm depending upon you
To perk up and give me
A nice thaw and not
Another surprise snowfall.

Let me replace my sunlamp
With the actual sun
And let me go the distance
Without frying up.

21. It's nearly fall.

The maple leaves are turning pink.
They're brightening into a red that cuts the sky, like striking a match.
The flame of fall.
The patterned quilt of leaves tuck in the valley.
Making ready for winter.

The chill caresses your neck and cheeks, tugs on your scarf.
The simmering sun has broken its solitary hold and paints a shimmering hue on the moon.

Your gloved fingernails tug a little harder on the folds of your knitted cap.
The cotton stitches almost cover your eyes.

There's rhythm in the crisp footfalls against fallen leaves and crunched beer cans.
Perhaps even a spirit in the exhales of chilled air.

It's the season of ghosts and enchantments.
But advertising misplaces natural wonder for superhuman thrills.

If you haven't felt the heartbeat in the trails,
go to the overgrown spaces between neighborhoods.
Get out of that paved loop.
Interrupt the relentless efficiency, and the chemicals that
quicken
as soon as another task
gets ticked off.

Rest in that even pace, something you can breathe into.
You don't need to push yourself when your body
breathes itself,
and can soothe itself without needing to cling
so tightly.

If anything, fall teaches you that it is the falling apart
that lays the groundwork
for our eventual rise.

To grow, one needs to shed what's already dead.
Crunch those red leaves,
tie your laces, and leave behind what haunts
you–

the you that never even existed in the first place.

www.ingramcontent.com/pod-product-compliance
Lightning Source LLC
Chambersburg PA
CBHW051735130826
49812CB00033B/877
9789370926059